GARRY KASPAROV

checkmate!

my first chess book

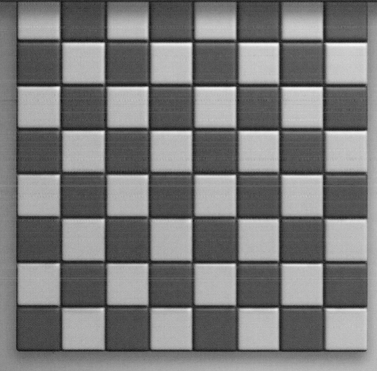

contents

EVERYMAN CHESS

First published in 2004 by Gloucester Publishers plc
Northburgh House, 10 Northburgh Street, London EC1V 0AT

Copyright ©2004 Everyman Chess
Reprinted 2012

British Library Cataloguing-in-Publication Data
A catalogue record for this book is available
from the British Library. ISBN 978-1-85744-358-5

Distributed in North America by
The Globe Pequot Press, P.O Box 480,
246 Goose Lane, Guilford, CT 06437-0480

All other sales enquiries should be directed to
Everyman Chess, Northburgh House,
10 Northburgh Street, London EC1V 0AT
tel: 020 7253 7887 fax: 020 7490 3708
email: info@everymanchess.com
www.everymanchess.com

Editor: Byron Jacobs
Design, typesetting and illustrations: Horatio Monteverde
Printed and bound in Estonia

checkmate!

You'll have hours of real fun when you learn to play chess, the most popular board game in the world.

Checkmate! will teach you how the pieces move and what they're worth. You'll quickly learn how to attack and defend and how to win your first game, your first checkmate!

Start to play immediately. I'll teach you about tactics and strategy and soon you'll be playing with your friends and family, at home, at school or even on the internet.

I hope you enjoy these first lessons of this wonderful game.

Good Luck !

Garry Kasparov

playing the game

Chess is a war game.
You and your opponent control
an identical army of pieces.
To win the game you will have to
use your army more effectively
than your opponent.

The two sides in chess
are White and Black.
The 'White' player plays with
the light-coloured pieces and
the 'Black' player plays with
the dark-coloured ones.

The chessboard is the battlefield for
your game. The board is made up
of 64 squares arranged 8 x 8.
The squares are coloured
alternately light
and dark. When
you set up the
board, you should be
careful that the square in
the bottom right hand corner
(from the white player's point
of view) is light-coloured.

The chess pieces – your army –
are always set out the same way
at the start of the game.

The two players move
alternately and White has the
tiny advantage of having the first
move. If it is your turn to move, you
must move – passing is not allowed.

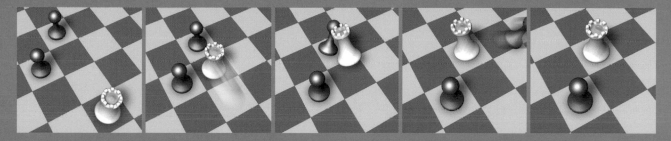

The chess pieces all move in different ways. To make a move, you pick up one of your pieces and relocate it to a new square. You cannot move a piece to a square already occupied by one of your pieces. However, you can move to a square occupied by an opponent's piece. This piece is then 'captured' and is removed from the board.

The ultimate aim of the game is to deliver checkmate – the equivalent of capturing the opposing king. Sometimes neither side can breach the other's defences and the game ends as a draw. In games between strong players this is quite common.

what you need to know

The chessboard must be set up with a light square in the lower right hand corner, from White's point of view.

White moves first and then the players move alternately. You must make a move, you cannot 'pass'.

The initial position is the same for each game.

When you capture an opponent's piece it is removed from the board and takes no further part in the action.

The aim of the game is to deliver checkmate – to capture the opponent's king. It is also possible for the game to end as a draw.

pieces and initial positions

Each player in chess starts with an
identical army of sixteen pieces:

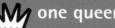

one queen

The queen is your most powerful piece
– take good care of her! Note where the
queens start the game – White's is on a
white square and Black's on a dark square.

one king

The king is the most important piece.
Lose the king and you lose the game!
So remember to protect it well.

two bishops

The bishop is the only piece which cannot
reach all the squares on the board.
One bishop can only ever move on the light
squares, the other only on the dark squares.

two knights

The knight is the only piece which
can 'hop' over other pieces.

two rooks

The rook is the easiest piece to understand.
It simply moves in straight lines – up and
down or side to side.

elements of the board:

ranks
ranks are the lines across the board

files
files are the lines running up the board

It is very important to remember how to set up the pieces.

Each side's pieces start on the back two rows, but they will not stay there for long. As the game warms up, the pieces quickly come out, and the fighting begins!

Two common mistakes made by players new to the game are:

Getting the king and queen the wrong way round

Setting up the board the wrong way round so that the square in the right hand corner is a dark square instead of a light one.

eight pawns
The pawn is the lowliest of all the chess pieces. All the same, it has the potential for great things - only pawns can be 'promoted' to become other pieces.

what you need to know

There are six different chess pieces: king, queen, rook, bishop, knight and pawn.

Each side starts the game with a total of 16 pieces.

The starting position is the same for every game.

 the rook

The rook moves in a very straightforward manner – in straight lines along the files and the ranks.

We will start with the easiest of all the pieces to understand – the rook.

The rook is the second most powerful piece – stronger than the knight and the bishop, but weaker than the queen. The rooks and the queens are known as major pieces.

From this position the rook can move to any of the indicated squares.

As the rook cannot 'jump' over pieces, its movement here is slightly restricted. It cannot move to h7, h8, a5 or b5. However, it can capture the knight on c5. The rook cannot 'capture' the pawn on h6 – you can **never** capture your own pieces.

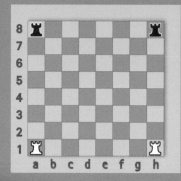

Each player starts
with two rooks:
a8 and h8 for Black
a1 and h1 for White

value: 5 points

strengths:
the rook is strong in open
positions and endgames.

weaknesses:
the rook does not
operate so well when
the position is blocked.

master tips for the rook

The rook is the second most powerful piece.

In the early stages of the game it is usually best
to keep the rooks on the back rank.

Always look for opportunities to place your rooks
on open files. An open file is a file which does not
have any pawns on it. A rook on an open file often
has opportunities to create havoc by advancing
deep into the opponent's position.

Rooks can become very strong in the endgame.

With just a king and rook you can force
checkmate against a lone king.

the bishop

The bishop moves along diagonal lines. Like the rook, it can move freely as long as there are no other pieces blocking its path.

The bishop's value is about the same as the knight's but it is much weaker than the queen. The bishops and knights are called the minor pieces.

In the first diagram the bishop can move to any of the marked squares. Like the rook and all the other pieces except the knight, the bishop cannot jump over pieces.

Sometimes a bishop can be badly blocked in as you can see in the diagram below. As we will see later, these white pawns are blocked by the black ones and cannot move. Therefore they are blocking their own bishop. A bishop that is stuck like this is often called a 'bad bishop'. Try to avoid having one!

So, in the second diagram, the bishop cannot move to a4, e2 or f1, but it can capture the rook on e2. Remember - you can **never** capture your own pieces. This is why the bishop cannot move to a4.

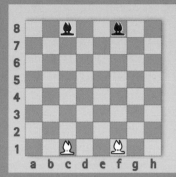

Each player starts
with two bishops:
c8 and f8 for Black
c1 and f1 for White

value: 3 points

strengths:
the bishop is strong in open
positions on long diagonals.

weaknesses:
the bishop struggles when the
position is blocked or when it
is restricted by pawns fixed on
squares of the same colour.

master tips for the bishop

The bishop, along with the knight, is the least
powerful piece (not counting pawns!).

Bishops and knights are known
as the minor pieces.

The bishop does very well in open positions,
but less well when it is blocked in.

You cannot give checkmate with just a king
and bishop against a lone king, but you can
with two bishops, or with a bishop
and knight.

♛ the queen

The queen has the powers of the rook and the bishop put together. You already know how those two pieces move, and so understanding how the queen moves will be easy.

The queen is the key player in your army. It is the most powerful piece and can cause havoc, especially if it gets near the enemy king. However, because it is so valuable, you must use it carefully. It's worth almost as much as two rooks. The queens and rooks are called the major pieces.

In the first diagram the queen stands in the middle of the board and can move to any of the marked squares - a total of 27 possible moves. This is almost half the squares on the chessboard. No doubt about it - the queen is a mighty piece. But remember that, as with rooks and bishops, she cannot jump over other pieces and this limits her mobility. We see this in the second diagram.

It is easy to be carried away by the power of the queen and to want to bring her into the game as soon as possible. Be careful, though. At the beginning of the game when there are many pieces on the board, the queen can easily be attacked. It is usually better to be patient and keep her safely behind the other pieces and pawns for a while.

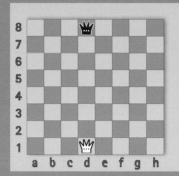

Each player starts with one queen: d1 for White and d8 for Black

master tips for the queen

The queen is the most powerful piece.
The queens and rooks are the major pieces.

The queen is a very strong attacking piece. When the queens are exchanged – that is, both queens have been captured – there is much less danger of a checkmating attack.

Early in the game it is best to be cautious with your queen. The queen becomes much stronger after some minor pieces have been exchanged.

You can checkmate easily with a king and queen against a lone king. This is a very important skill which you will learn later in this book.

value: 9 points

strengths:
the queen is strong in open positions and can be very powerful in an attack.

weaknesses:
because the queen is so valuable you must be careful not to expose her too much.

the knight

A knight is worth about the same as a bishop. Bishops and knights are called minor pieces.

Here are three different ways to explain how the knight moves - choose the one that is easiest for you to picture in your mind.

The knight moves in an L-shape - two squares along a rank or file and then one square to the side.

Imagine a box - three squares by two squares. The knight moves from one corner to the opposite one.

The knight hops around and this special movement makes it a very important and difficult piece.

Imagine a box - five squares by five with the knight in the middle. It can move to any square at the edge of the box that it would not be able to move to if it were a queen. Here it has a maximum of eight possible moves.

The knight is the only piece that is allowed to hop over other pieces, so in the next diagram it can move to the four marked squares, even though other pieces are in the way.

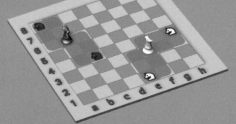

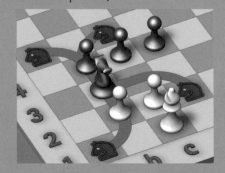

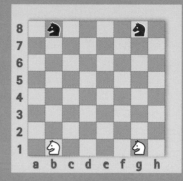

Each player starts
with two knights:
b8 and g8 for Black
b1 and g1 for White

value: 3 points

strengths:
the knight's special ability to hop
over other pieces makes it valuable
in blocked positions.

weaknesses:
knights are weak pieces when they
are away from the centre and have
fewer possible squares to move to.

master tips for the knight

The knight is worth about the same as a bishop.
The bishops and knights are called minor pieces.

Knights are very useful in blocked positions and
are at their best when they are in or near the
centre. The knight's first move should usually be
towards the centre, for example Nb1-c3, Ng1-f3,
Nb8-c6 or Ng8-f6.

You cannot checkmate with just a king and a
knight against a lone king. In fact, you cannot
checkmate even with two knights together
without other pieces to help.

♟ the pawn

Pawns are the foot soldiers of chess.

They can only move a very short distance. However, pawns have an extraordinary ability – to 'promote' when they reach the opponent's back rank. This power is one of the most important features of the game – overlook it at your peril!

Pawns are often called by the letter of the file they are standing on. For example, a pawn on the b-file is a b-pawn and a pawn on the f-file is an f-pawn.

the pawn move

In an ordinary move, a pawn simply moves one square up the board (away from its player). You can only move a pawn one square at a time unless it is still standing on its starting square. In that special case you can, if you want to, move it two squares forward. You can **never** move a pawn backwards.

the pawn capture

Pawns capture by moving one square forwards, but this time diagonally, to the left or to the right.

The white pawn on b3 can capture the black knight on a4 or the rook on c4. The black pawn on f6 can capture the white pawns on e5 or g5. It cannot capture the white pawn on f5 which is blocking its path up the board.

The black pawn on f7 (again, on its original square) can move to f6 or f5 and the pawn on h4 can move to h3.

Here the white b-pawn (which is on its original square) can move to b3 or b4 and the pawn on d4 can only move to d5.

Each player starts
with eight pawns:
a7 to h7 for Black
a2 to h2 for White

value: 1 point

strengths:
pawns can act as a shield for the king early in the game. They are also very important in the endgame as they can promote to a queen if they reach the opponent's back rank.

weaknesses:
pawns can often be quite weak and feeble, especially if they become separated from one another or if they become 'doubled' (when two pawns are on the same file).

master tips for the pawn

The pawn is the only chess piece which captures in a different way to its ordinary move.

Pawns can only ever move forwards, so you have to be very careful when you make pawn moves. Remember that if things get sticky, you will not be able to reverse out of trouble!

It is nearly always a good idea to place pawns in the centre of the board early in the game. It is especially important to try to move the e- and d-pawns. These pawns can control the centre and moving them opens up files and diagonals so that the bishops and queen can be developed, that is, moved forward to take part in the battle.

two unusual pawn moves

There are two special facts about the pawns that you need to know. They are:

● **Pawns can promote.**

● **Pawns can capture en passant.**

pawn promotion

Pawn promotion is a really important idea in chess. The basic idea is that, if a pawn reaches the opponent's back rank, it can be replaced with any piece, except a king. We say the pawn has 'promoted'. You can choose any piece you like to replace the pawn but, since the queen is the most powerful piece, it is nearly always chosen.

Here is an example to show how pawn promotion works.

White, with only a king and a pawn, seems to have no hope of being able to checkmate the black king. But, by playing his pawn from g7 to g8, he can get it to the back rank and promote it to another piece. He will choose a queen to replace the pawn and can then (as we shall see later) easily checkmate the black king in a few moves.

In the diagram above the white pawn on c7 can promote either by moving to c8, or by capturing the knight on d8.

The black pawn on e2 has just one way to reach the back rank – by capturing the rook on d1.

The idea of turning a pawn into a queen is so fantastic that some new players try to move their pawns up the board as quickly as they possibly can. Unfortunately, when there are a lot of pieces still on the board, you are more likely to lose your pawn than to promote it. Advancing pawns a long way up the board is more effective in the endgame when there are fewer enemy pieces about.

en passant

The en passant (French for 'in passing') rule is a funny one which confuses many beginners. The rule says that if your opponent's pawn moves two squares from its starting position then you may capture it with one of your pawns (not with a piece) as if it had moved just one square. However, you can only make this capture on the very next move. If you choose to make another move then the chance for the en passant capture is gone. It is easy to see this with the help of a diagram.

This is now the position. White can capture Black's b-pawn as if it had moved just one square – to b6.

White has captured the pawn.

Black to play. Black advances his b-pawn two squares, moving it from b7 to b5

what you need to know

The fact that pawns can promote by reaching the back rank is absolutely basic to the game of chess. If there were no such thing as promotion then almost all endgames would finish as draws.

Moving pawns forward, trying to promote them, is more likely to work in the endgame than in the early stages of the game.

En passant is a peculiar, but important rule. Make sure you understand it now, so you won't get caught out later!

the king

The king is your most valuable piece
and you must guard it well. Losing the
king – checkmate – means losing the
game. One of your most important jobs
early in the game will be to make a
safe shelter for your king.

The king is never exchanged from the board and so
it has no trading value. However, if it did, it would
be worth about the same as a bishop or knight.

Learning how the king moves is easy. It simply
moves one square – and one square only –
in any direction, along a file, rank or diagonal.

In this diagram the white king has six possible
moves and can also capture the black bishop.
The black king, at the edge of the board, is more
restricted and has just five possible moves.

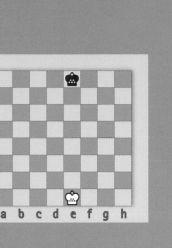

Each player starts
with one king:
e8 for Black
e1 for White

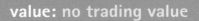

value: no trading value

strengths:
the king can be a very strong piece in the endgame, when there are fewer pieces on the board and less danger of a snap checkmate.

weaknesses:
in the opening and middlegame, getting the king safe is very important. Countless games have been lost, even by very strong players, when they have forgotten this simple rule.

master tips for the king

The king cannot be exchanged but, in an endgame, its powers of movement make it worth about the same as a knight or bishop.

The king is the key piece in chess. The ultimate aim of the game is to checkmate your opponent's king and to stop this from happening to yours.

Check and checkmate are very important ideas in chess – see page 24.

an important move: castling

When you castle, you move your king two squares from its starting square, either to the left or to the right. For White this means that the king moves from e1 to either g1 or c1. The rook which is nearest to the king then hops over the king and lands on the next square. For White this is d1 or f1.

three important rules about castling:

- Your king and rook must both be on their starting squares, and neither of them must have moved during the game. There must not be any pieces between the king and rook.

- You cannot castle if you are in check.

- You cannot castle if it means that you will move your king through a check.

White can castle.

White has castled **kingside.**

White has castled **queenside.**

Here Black cannot castle queenside as the king is in check (from the white knight).

Here White cannot castle kingside as his king would have to pass over the f1 square which is attacked by the black bishop.

why castling is important

This is the kind of position that you will often find after the first few moves of a game.

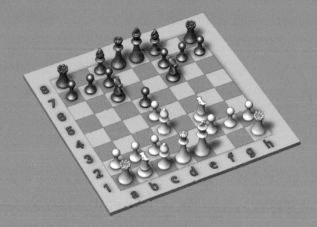

White solves both these problems by castling.

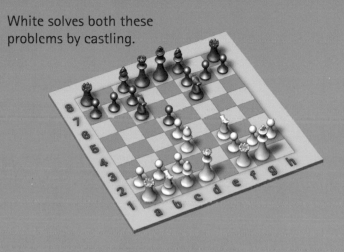

after White has castled

We shall look at opening play in more detail later in the book, but here I would like you to think about just two important principles:

- **Develop your pieces.**
- **Get your king to safety.**

Now the king has a safe haven behind a wall of pawns. Meanwhile the rook is ready to join in the game. It is not doing much at the moment but it could soon move to e1 where it would be active along the e-file.

If you look at White's position in the above diagram you can see that he will have little trouble developing the queen, the bishops and the knights – all of these have clear lines to join in the game. But the rooks are buried away in the corners – how on earth will they ever join in? And how can White make sure his king is safe?

what you need to know

Castling is the only occasion when you move two pieces at the same time.

There are three important rules about castling – learn them!

Castling is important because it helps to bring a rook into the game and make the king secure.

check and checkmate

checkmate

The word 'checkmate' comes from an Arabic phrase meaning 'the king is dead'. But the strange thing about chess is that the king never in fact dies. Instead of actually taking your opponent's king, you only need to attack it so that it cannot escape and would be captured on the next move. When a king cannot avoid being taken in the next move, then we say it is 'checkmated' and the game is over.

check

When your king is threatened by an enemy piece you are 'in check' and you must escape from the check on your very next move. The simplest way to do this is to move the king to a safe square.

Here are some examples of check. In all cases, the safe squares for the king are shown.

The king is in check from the rook and the rook covers (is attacking) the squares e8 and g8 on the back rank. However, the king can move up the board as shown.

The white king is in check from the knight, which also covers the d2-square. However, there are still four squares that the king could move to.

It is not just the checking piece which can cover squares around the king. Other pieces can help, as we see in the following examples.

The white bishop (giving check), knight and king cover a total of six squares. Black has just two escape squares. In the lower diagram, the white king has just one. Note that the two kings can never stand right next to each other as then they would both be in check. This is not allowed, because you must never move your king into check.

other ways to deal with a check

There are two other ways to deal with a check:

● **You can capture the checking piece.**

● **You can put a piece of your own in the way to block the check.** This is called 'interposing' a piece. Here is an example:

White is in check from the black rook. As we have seen, there are three possible ways to deal with this check and all of them are possible here:

Move the king to a safe square – in this case d2.

Capture the checking piece. Here White can take the rook on e5 with the bishop on b2.

Block the check. Here White can do this by playing the rook from b3 to e3.

If we now change the position slightly by adding a black pawn on c3, the situation is very different.

Now White cannot deal with the check in any of the three ways:

The pawn is attacking the d2-square, so there is no safe move for the white king.

The pawn is stopping the bishop from capturing the rook.

The pawn is stopping the white rook from moving from b3 to e3.

White has been checkmated! The game is over and Black wins.

what you need to know

A check is a forcing move. You must deal with a check on your very next move – you are not allowed to ignore it.

There are three ways to meet a check:

● Move the king to a safe square.

● Capture the checking piece.

● Block the check.

If none of these is possible, then the position is checkmate.

try it yourself

The following puzzles will test your knowledge of how the pieces move. Think about each position carefully and try to answer the questions before looking up the answers.

1 Identify all the possible moves and captures that can be made by:

a. The white bishop on e3.

b. The black rook on g6.

2 Identify all the possible moves and captures that can be made by:

a. The white queen on b3.

b. The black knight on f6.

3 This is a well-known opening position:

a. Find all the pieces (not pawns) which currently have no legal moves.

b. Find the three pieces on the board which have precisely **one** legal move.

4 We know that the players move alternately. However, for the sake of this puzzle assume that only White moves.

a. How can the bishop on e5 capture the black pawn on a3 in two moves?

b. How can the knight on f3 capture the black rook on h8 in three moves?

c. How can the rook on e1 capture the black bishop on a8 in three moves?

5 In this position each side has three pawns. Identify the possible moves and captures for each pawn.

7 If it is White's move here, can he castle kingside or queenside?

8 If it is Black's move here, can he castle kingside or queenside?

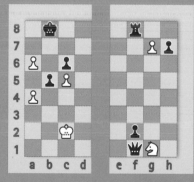

6 The black pawn has just advanced from b7 to b5.

a. White now has two possible pawn captures. What are they?

b. What options are available to: the white pawn on g7; the black pawn on f2. What will happen after either of these pawns moves?

9

10

11

12

In these four positions the king is either:

a. Not in check.

b. Has been checkmated.

c. In check.

Which is correct in each case?

chess notation

A tremendous feature of chess is the ability to write down the moves of a game while it is being played. If you play a game against a computer then the ever-helpful machine will usually record the game for you. However, if you are playing against a friend you can, if you wish, record the moves yourself.

There are many good reasons to do this. If you have played a beautiful game you may wish to play over it again at your leisure. If you are serious about improving your play then, with a record of the game, you can look over it later and try to see what you did right and wrong, possibly with the help of a coach. There is also a huge amount of chess literature to be found in newspapers, magazines, books and on the web. In order to access this material you need to understand chess notation.

Fortunately, chess notation isn't complicated and can be picked up easily.

By now you will be familiar with the chessboard and the labelling of the squares.

To record a move you simply write down the symbol of the piece followed by the square it has moved to.

The 'symbol' of the piece is the initial letter or, in the case of the knight, 'N', so as not to be confused with the king. Sometimes in chess publications a 'figurine' is used. This is an actual symbol of the piece.

Piece	Symbol	Figurine
King	K	♔
Queen	Q	♕
Rook	R	♖
Bishop	B	♗
Knight	N	♘

In this diagram, if the white queen moves to the square marked with the dot we write Qb6. Or if the knight moves to the square marked with a cross we write Nc3.

The exception to this rule is when a pawn moves. In this case we only write down the square that the pawn moves to. So on the right hand side of the diagram, White can play h5 and Black can play e5. Note that we do not write Ph5 and Pe5. The 'P' is irrelevant as, if you think about it, you will see that only one pawn can ever move to a particular square and so there is no confusion.

Sometimes a piece is captured. In that case we insert an 'x' between the symbol and the square.

For example White can play Bxd5 and Black can play Nxc2. If a pawn capture is made, we write down the file from which the pawn has just moved. White can play cxb3 and Black can play bxc2.

Sometimes a move is check. In that case we add a '+' at the end of the move. So if it is White's move (on the right hand side of the diagram) he can play Rf7+ or Rh5+. Black can play Nxh3+ (note that this is also a capture).

what you need to know

To record a move you write the symbol for the piece followed by the square to which it moves. The exception is for pawn moves, when only the square the pawn moves to is required.

When a piece is captured, insert an 'x'.

When a move gives check add an '+' on the end of the move.

more on notation

There are three other things you need to know to master chess notation.

Castling kingside is written as 0-0 and castling queenside as 0-0-0

Here White can play 0-0-0 and Black can play 0-0.

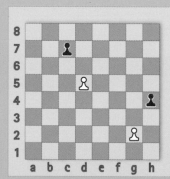

If an en passant capture is made then the move is written as if the pawn had only advanced one square and then been captured. In this diagram Black plays c5 and White can then play dxc6. Alternatively if White plays g4 Black can reply hxg3.

When pawn promotion occurs you add the symbol for the promoted piece. In the following diagram White could play c8Q or cxb8Q. Black could play f1N (note that this gives checkmate and so is one of the rare cases when it is better not to promote to a queen!)

Now play through the following sequence, starting from the initial position.

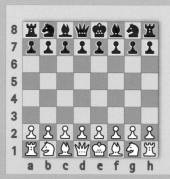

1	e4 e5
2	Nf3 Nc6
3	d4

This opening is called the Scotch Game.

3	... exd4
4	Nxd4 Bb4+
5	Nc3 Nf6
6	Nxc6 bxc6
7	Bd3 0-0
8	0-0 Bb7
9	Be3 Qe7
10	Qe2 Rfe8

Points to note:

The figures at the start of each line simply indicate the move number.

After White's third move we have written a note and the game then resumes with Black's third move. To make it clear that this is a black move we insert '..' before the move.

On the tenth move Black moved a rook to e8. This is a slight problem as either black rook could have moved to e8 and so writing simply 'Re8' would not make the move clear. Therefore we indicate which rook had moved by identifying the file from which it had moved, i.e. Rfc8 – meaning the rook from the f-file has moved. Occasionally even this may not work. Perhaps two rooks are on the c-file and both can move to c4. In that case we use the rank and write, for example, R6c4.

If you have played all the moves correctly you should now have the following position on the board.

It is also possible to indicate the strength (or weakness) of a move by adding symbol(s) after the move, as follows:

!	Good move
!!	Brilliant move
?	Bad move
??	Blunder
!?	Interesting move
?!	Dubious move

what you need to know

Castling kingside is written as **0–0** and castling queenside as **0–0–0**

En passant captures are written as if the pawn had just advanced one square.

When there is a black move with no initial white move (after a note) we insert '...'

If a move is ambiguous, we add the file (or rank) that the piece has moved from.

winning

resigning

The usual way that a game ends between players learning the game is by checkmate. However, at a higher level, this almost never happens. This is because there nearly always comes a point in the game when eventual defeat becomes inevitable and playing on is futile. This may be because an obvious checkmate is looming, or possibly because a player has lost so much material that there is no chance to fight back. At this stage a player can 'resign' the game, either by simply saying 'I resign' or, more dramatically, by tipping over the king.

You should never be too keen to resign. After all, it means you sacrifice any further tiny chances you might have in the game. However, when you recognise that the position really is hopeless then it is better to give up rather than sit around and wait for the inevitable execution.

Here is a typical example:

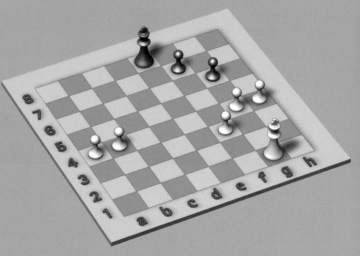

Here White is three pawns up in an endgame. As we already know, when pawns reach the opponent's back rank they can promote to a queen. White will have no trouble achieving this goal here and then will checkmate easily with the new queen. Although Black can struggle on here for many moves, it just isn't worth it. There is no possibility for White to make a mistake which would be serious enough to jeopardise his winning chances. It is best to resign and concentrate on the next game.

winning on time

Virtually all serious chess is played with a chess clock. Usually, you have a certain allocated amount of time to complete a number of moves. You should know how many moves you have made, because you will be writing the moves down on a scoresheet. A typical 'time control' is 40 moves in two hours. If you do not complete the required number of moves in time then you have 'lost on time' and the game is over. Even if you are about to play your 40th move, which will give checkmate, it does not matter. If you have only made 39 moves when time is up, then you lose immediately.

The classical form of a chess clock actually has a 'flag' which is raised by the hour hand as it approaches '12'. When the hand passes the hour mark, the flag 'falls', indicating that time is up. However, in modern play digital clocks are now becoming increasingly common.

what you need to know

When your position becomes hopeless and there is no real possibility of your opponent making a mistake – it is best to resign.

When you play games, at whatever speed, with a clock, be careful not to run 'short of time'. If your flag falls before you complete the right number of moves – then you automatically lose the game.

drawing

drawing

There are three basic ways a game can be drawn.

stalemate

If one side has no possible moves, but the king is not in check, then the position is stalemate. This becomes crucial in numerous endgame positions. Here are some typical stalemates which can occur in endgames.

Black to move: White has been hoping to promote his b-pawn to a queen and then give checkmate. Unfortunately, it is Black's move and the position is stalemate.

Black to move: Even with an extra piece, White has been unable to promote the pawn and again the result is a draw by stalemate.

White to move: Black has blundered! While trying to checkmate with king and queen he has accidentally stumbled into a stalemate.

White to move: Even when one side has a piece or two the game can sometimes be drawn by stalemate. Here the white bishop cannot move (the king will be in check) and he has no moves with the king either.

perpetual check

Sometimes, one side can launch an attack, but it proves to be insufficient to give checkmate. However, there is an opportunity to create endless checks from which the opposing king can never escape. The result is 'perpetual check' and a draw.

Here is a position from a game between two British players William Watson (White) and Julian Hodgson (Black), played at Reykjavik in 1989. White has tried an attack but it has not been successful and he is now in some difficulties.

However, he played
1 Rxg6+ fxg6
2 Qxg6+ Kh8.

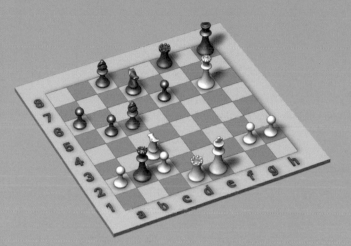

Here is a typical position where a draw can be agreed.

Now he played **3 Qh6+ Kg8 4 Qg6+**. Although White cannot quite give checkmate, the checks will go on forever and so the game is a draw.

agreeing a draw

At any stage during the game, one player can 'offer' a draw. Their opponent then has the option of accepting, or continuing to try and win the game. It is important to know the correct behaviour for offering a draw: you should say 'I offer a draw', at the same time as you make your move. You should not offer a draw while it is your turn to move, nor should you offer a draw while your opponent is thinking about their move. Draws are normally agreed because the position has become too simple and balanced for there to be any opportunity of either player forcing a win.

Material is completely equal and both sides have a solid position. There is no real chance for any complications to occur. If the game continues then the two sides will most likely just move their pieces around with no purpose. In such situations, it is better to agree a draw and get on with the next game.

what you need to know

Stalemate occurs when one side has no legal moves, but is not in check.

Sometimes it is possible for one player to give an endless series of repeating checks. If they choose to do this, the game is drawn by perpetual check.

At any stage during a game you can offer a draw. If your opponent agrees, then the game is 'drawn by agreement'.

the values

We have already seen that the pieces are not all equal. Some are more powerful than others and thus have greater value. Here is a reminder of their relative value.

Pawn – 1 unit

Knights and bishops – 3 units

Rook – 5 units

Queen – 9 units

Although the ultimate aim of the game is to deliver checkmate, this is not how most games are decided. Most games are decided when one side makes a significant gain in material and this advantage is slowly nursed to victory. Gaining material, or at least avoiding losing it, should be your priority in the early part of the game.

why do we need more material?

Hopefully, this should be obvious. If you are in charge of an army, would you rather have ten soldiers and your opponent five, or the other way round? The situation is not quite so clear cut in chess as the pieces have different values. However the basic principle applies. If you have more pieces, or better quality pieces than your opponent, you have a much greater chance to win the game.

The advantage in material does not have to be huge. At a high level, players are so skilled at winning with small advantages that games are often resigned after the loss of just a pawn.

relative values

The following are all more or less equivalent:

- Bishops and knights are about equal.
- A bishop or knight is worth about three pawns.

$$\text{bishop} = \text{knight} = \text{pawn pawn pawn}$$

- A rook is worth a minor piece plus two pawns.

$$\text{rook} = \text{bishop or knight} + \text{pawn pawn}$$

- A bishop and knight equal a rook and a pawn.

$$\text{bishop} + \text{knight} = \text{rook} + \text{pawn}$$

- Two rooks are equal to a queen and a pawn.

$$\text{rook} + \text{rook} = \text{queen} + \text{pawn}$$

practical play

Knowing the values of the pieces allows us to make good decisions when faced with the prospect of various captures during a game.

Here is an example. White is a piece down, but has four possible captures. Can you find them and say which one is the best?

1 Rxb7 – White wins a bishop.

1 Rxe7 – White wins a knight.

1 Qxb4 – White wins a rook.

1 Nxg4! – White wins the prize piece – black's queen. The best move.

The situation becomes more complicated when you can take a piece but your opponent can then recapture. Then you need to do some basic maths to see if the trade is good for you.

Here White has five possible captures but only one of them is good:

1 Bxg7? White captures a pawn but this is bad as Black replies 1 ... Kxg7 and White loses a bishop for a pawn (1 – 3 = -2)

1 Rxe8+? This is also bad. Black replies 1 ... Qxe8 and White has lost a rook for a bishop (3 – 5 = -2)

1 Qxg6? This is disastrous. Black replies 1 ... fxg6, and White has lost a whole queen for a mere knight (3 – 9 = -6)

1 Qxc8. This is okay. Black will recapture, 1 ... Rxc8, and the queens have been exchanged with no advantage to either side (9 – 9 = 0)

1 Bxa8! This is best. Black can recapture, 1 ... Qxa8, but White has gained rook for bishop (5 – 3 = +2)

what you need to know

It is essential to know the values of the pieces – commit the table to memory.

Checkmate ends the game but the turning point in most games comes when one side loses material.

It is very important to make captures and exchanges which favour you in material terms.

more on piece values

when your pieces are threatened

When it is your turn to move you must look carefully around the board to see if there is any immediate danger to your own pieces. To achieve a reasonable standard of play in chess it is essential that you are able to spot threats quickly and to decide if they are dangerous or not.

In this position there are various potential 'threats' against the white pieces. Let us consider each in turn.

The knight on e4 is threatened by the black bishop on b7. However, it is protected by the white rook on e1 so 1 ... Bxe4 can be met by 2 Rxe4. Bishop and knight are equal in value and so this is fine for White.

The rook on e1 is threatened by the black queen. However, it is protected by the white queen on d1 so 1 ... Qxe1+ can be met by 2 Qxe1. The queen is far more valuable than the rook, so this exchange would greatly benefit White.

The bishop on a3 is threatened by the black queen. This piece is not protected and White must do something about it. A good, safe move is 1 Bb2, removing the bishop from danger.

Here is another example. Try to work it out for yourself before reading the text.

The knight on f3 is threatened by the black rook on f8. However, it is protected by the white queen on e2 and the pawn on g2. A rook is more valuable than a knight so there is no danger there.

The bishop on d3 is threatened by the black queen. However, it is protected by the white queen on e2 so 1 ... Qxd3 can be met by 2 Qxd3. Clearly this would be a disaster for Black.

The rook on c4 is threatened by the black bishop. It is protected by the white bishop on d3, but this does not help, as a rook is much more valuable than a bishop. White must pay attention to this threat. A good move is 1 R4c2, getting the rook away from danger.

dealing with threats

Sometimes you find that one of your pieces is threatened, but you are not keen to move it. If the piece that is attacking it is of greater value, you can consider protecting your piece. Here is an example.

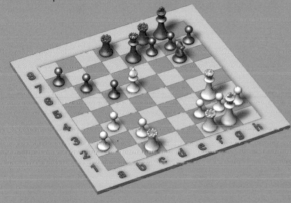

The white bishop on d5 is threatened by the black rook. However, the bishop is on a good central square and so, rather than moving it, White can protect it with 1 c4. The bishop is now firmly anchored in the centre.

Another way to deal with an attack is to block it, as in the following posiiton.

The white queen is threatened by the bishop on e6. Moving the queen is fine but perhaps better is 1 Bc4, which gets a piece into the game as well as blocking the threat.
Now 1 ... Bxc4 is met by 2 Qxc4.
Also possible is 1 c4, which blocks the attack with a pawn.

what you need to know

It is important to develop the skill of quickly spotting threats to your pieces.

Often it is necessary to move the attacked piece to a safe square.

If you do not want to be 'chased away', look for chances to protect your attacked piece (if the piece threatening it is of greater value) or to block the attack.

the fork

Many of your moves in a chess game will create a threat, such as a check or an attack against an unprotected enemy piece. In normal circumstances your opponent may well be able to deal with such a threat.

However, if you can create two threats at once, your opponent could be in trouble. You can only make one move at a time and so it might not be possible to deal with two threats at the same time. A move which creates two threats is called a fork.

The most common example of a fork – and often the most difficult to deal with – is when one of the 'threats' is a threat to the enemy king, i.e. a check.

what you need to know

A fork occurs when you create two threats with one move.

All pieces can create forks, but knights and pawns are especially good at it.

Watch out for unprotected pieces (both yours and your opponent's). These can be vulnerable to forks.

One of the best pieces for creating forks is the knight. In this example White plays **1 Ne7+**. The knight on e7 checks the king on g8 whilst also threatening the black queen on g6. Black must move the king and then White will capture the black queen for a mere knight which will result in an easy victory.

Here are some other examples of forks:

a pawn fork

Black has placed the knight and bishop on clumsy squares and now, after **1 e4**, the knight and bishop are forked – Black will lose a piece for just a pawn.

a bishop fork

Here Black's king and queen find themselves unhappily aligned on the a2-g8 diagonal. White plays **1 Bd5+** and forks the king and queen. Note that the white bishop is protected by the knight on c3 so **1 ... Qxd5** is met by **2 Nxd5**. White wins the queen for just a bishop.

a queen fork

This position shows that even the best players in the world can sometimes overlook a fork. This position occurred in a game between the American grandmaster Larry Christiansen (playing White) and ex-world champion Anatoly Karpov (playing Black). Karpov has just developed his bishop to d6. This was revealed as a horrible blunder when his opponent replied **1 Qd1**, forking the knight on h5 and bishop on d6 and winning a clear piece. At this level, the gain of a piece is always decisive and Karpov resigned at once.

the pin

The pin is a very important tactical device. A pin occurs when a low value piece is unable to move because this would expose a higher value piece behind it. This higher value piece is often the king which, as we know, can never be left exposed to check. The piece that is caught in the trap is said to be 'pinned'.

Pins can only be carried out by pieces that move in a straight line: bishops, rooks and queens. Here are two typical examples. In each case the pin is against the king.

The black knight is pinned along the back rank against the king. The knight cannot move without exposing the king to check.

what you need to know

A pin occurs when a low value piece cannot move without exposing a higher value piece behind.

Only bishops, rooks and queens can pin pieces.

If you have created a pin yourself, look for ways to apply pressure to the pinned piece.

The white rook is pinned against the king by the black bishop. Again, the rook cannot move as this would result in a check to the king.

a harmless pin

Pins occur all the time. Quite often these pins are harmless as there is no great advantage in capturing the pinned piece.

This position occurs after 1 d4 Nf6 2 c4 e6 3 Nc3 Bb4. This opening is known as the Nimzo-Indian Defence. With the third move ... Bb4, Black has pinned the white knight on c3 against the king. However, this is not a problem for White. The knight and bishop are of equal value and so White should not be worried about Black capturing on c3, as long as he is able to recapture. At the moment the knight is protected by the pawn on b2. Black does not even have an immediate threat.
If White is nervous about the knight, it can always be protected further by a move such as **4 Qc2, 4 Qb3 or 4 Bd2**. All of these are good moves.

the power of the pin

You must be careful when a piece of yours is pinned. Your opponent may bring added pressure as in the following example.

Here White has just brought the queen to e2 and pinned the black knight against the king. White is threatening to capture the knight and so Black defends it with the move **1 ... d5**.
Now White uses the power of the pin with the move **2 d3**.

Now the black knight will be lost for just a pawn.

defending against a pin

The best way to deal with a pin is to break it. If in the previous example Black were to play **1 ... Qe7** (instead of 1 ... d5) we reach the following position.

1 ... Qe7 'breaks the pin' (the knight can now move without exposing the black king to check) and Black is okay.
If now **2 d3**, as before, then Black can safely reply **2 ... Nf6**.

Although White can capture the black queen, he will lose his own in the process.

the skewer

In the previous section we looked at the pin, where a low value piece is 'pinned' against a higher value piece. The skewer is the opposite of this. A high value piece is attacked and, if it moves away to escape capture, it exposes a piece behind. As with the pin, this high value piece is often the king.

As with the pin, skewers can only be carried out by bishops, rooks and queens. Let's look at some examples.

The white rook has given check. The black king must move and when it does, the queen on a7 will be lost.

what you need to know

A skewer occurs when a high value piece cannot move without exposing a low value piece behind. It is the reverse of a pin.

If one of your own pieces is skewered, try to move the attacked piece in such a way that it defends the threatened piece behind.

Only bishops, rooks and queens can create skewers.

The black bishop has given check on g4. The white king will have to move aside, and the white queen will perish.

A skewer does not have to involve the king. The queen is such a valuable piece that it can sometimes be the victim of a skewer.

defending against a skewer

If you find that your pieces have been skewered, look for a way to move the threatened piece in such a way that it can protect the vulnerable piece behind. Let's change the previous position very slightly, moving the black pawn from c7 to b7.

Here White plays **1 Bf3!** and, after the black queen moves, he will capture the rook on a8. Note that the white bishop is protected by the pawn on g2.

Now after **1 Bb4**, Black is skewered but can safely play **1 ... Rc7!**, defending the knight. If then **2 Bxe7**, Black keeps the balance with **2 ... Rxc7**.

One more example:

Here White plays **1 Bb4!** threatening the black rook. When it moves away, the knight on e7 will fall.

Black is in a skewer, but with the sneaky move **1 ... Qa7!**, the loose bishop on g7 can be protected.

try it yourself

In the following puzzles there are opportunities to make use the tactical ideas discussed in the previous three sections. Have a good go at solving the puzzles, looking for the right tactical ideas. Gaining a feel for how tactical ideas work in chess is a basic and crucial skill in chess.

1 Here White can play a successful fork with the knight. Can you see how?

3 How can White play a successful skewer?

2 Can you spot White's winning pin?

4 Here White has two different moves which will fork black pieces. One is successful and one not. Can you spot the moves and say which is which?

5 In the next six positions, White has a winning tactic in each case. It will be one of the three themes that we have been looking at: a fork, a pin or a skewer. Can you find them?

a.

c.

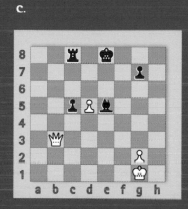

e.

b.

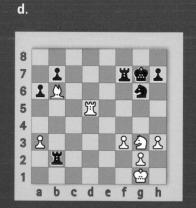

d.

f.

combining tactics

In the previous sections we have seen how it is possible to exploit the unfortunate positioning of the opponent's pieces with various tactical tricks. However, our opponents are not always quite so generous as to line themselves up for the knockout blow. Sometimes we have to give them a helping hand by luring their pieces onto vulnerable squares.

In this section we shall look at ways to set up winning tactics. This also gives us a better feel for how the pieces combine together.

what you need to know

If you cannot see an immediate tactical opportunity, look for a way to lure your opponent's pieces onto vulnerable squares.

Checking moves are particularly good as they are 'forcing' and the replies are often limited.

setting up a fork

This position occurred in the 1966 World Championship match between Tigran Petrosian (playing White) and Boris Spassky (Black). A piece count will reveal that White, although he has an extra pawn, is a rook for knight down. He can regain this immediately with 1 Nxf7 Kxf7 but he found a much better idea in the form of **1 Qh8+** which sets up a winning fork. After **1 ... Kxh8 2 Nxf7+** White goes on to capture the black queen and will be a piece up.

setting up a skewer

This position demonstrates a key theme in rook and pawn endgames. White would like to move the rook from a8 so that the pawn can then promote. However, Black is ready to capture this pawn with his own rook. So after **1 Rb8 Rxa7** the game will be a draw. However, White has the sneaky move **1 Rh8** and after **1 ... Rxa7...**

... he will continue **2 Rh7+** skewering the black rook. As we will see in the endgame section, king and rook can force checkmate against a lone king.

setting up a pin

Here is an example of how well a rook and knight can combine. White starts off with the clever **1 Rd8+**. Black can capture this rook with 1 ... Qxd8 but this runs into a fork with 2 Nf7+. So Black instead decides to ignore the bait and meets **1 Rd8+** with **1 ... Kg7**.

Now, however, **2 Rd7** creates a winning pin.

try it yourself

In this section we have ten puzzles where you have to try and find a way to set up a winning tactical blow with an earlier move. Be warned – some of these are quite tricky but please do have a good go at them before looking up the answer. Once you can do all these puzzles you will have a good grasp of how the pieces combine together.

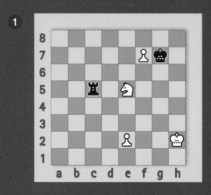

checkmate

Earlier, on pages 24–25, we looked at the various ways that a player can escape from check. As we already know, if a player cannot escape from check, then the position is checkmate, and the game is over.

In order to give checkmate, you must not only put the opposing king in check, you must also cover all of the possible flight squares.

It is good to attack with your major pieces (queen and rooks) which are more powerful and cover more squares than the minor pieces.

The white rook gives check and covers f8 and h8. The pawns block the advance of the black king.

The black queen gives check and covers f1, h1 and f2. Again the pawns block the king.

back rank checkmates

As we have already seen, it is usually good to castle early in the game to get the king safely behind a row of defensive pawns. However, this can lead to a 'weak back rank', where the arrival of a major piece on the back row can spell checkmate.

This time two rooks do the job.

This is a typical endgame position. The black king helps with the checkmate.

typical mating positions

In all of the following positions, note how powerful and effective the queen is for creating checkmates.

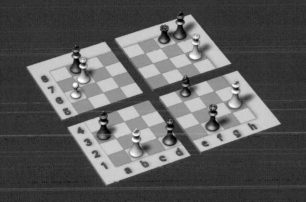

This position is from a game played in Amsterdam in 1987 between two Dutch players Ligterink (White) and Kuijf (Black).

White is attacking and one idea is 1 Nf7+. However, the black king could then move to g8 and White would not have made progress. Instead, White can sacrifice his queen to 'smother' the black king.

1 Qg8+! Rxg8 2 Nf7 checkmate.

smothered mate

Sometimes the opponent's pieces can accidentally contribute to this process by blocking possible escape squares for the king. Let's us look at an extreme example of this – a famous theme known as 'smothered mate'.

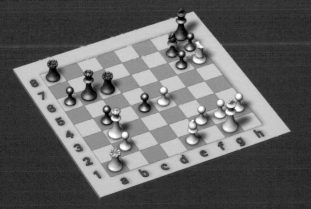

A beautiful finish: the black king finds itself suffocated by his own pieces.

what you need to know

The queen and rooks are very good at creating checkmating opportunities when they are near the opponent's king.

A 'weak back rank' can often create the possibility for a checkmate.

Sometimes 'friendly' pieces can block the king's escape squares.

basic checkmating patterns

Checkmating attacks are a very important element of chess. Many games are decided by a direct attack on the opponent's king. This may lead directly to a checkmate or, alternatively, the defending side may be forced to give up substantial material in order to fend off the threats. Either way, a well played attack can prove decisive.

In the previous section we looked at a few typical themes by which checkmate can arise. It is important to get a good feel for the ways that the pieces interact when combining to give checkmate. Much of the skill at chess is about recognising patterns and this is particularly important with checkmating positions.

Here we will go one step further and examine sequences which can lead to the kind of checkmating positions we looked at earlier.

the back rank

We have already seen how the king can get trapped on the back rank. Here are two examples which show how this can be exploited.

White seems to be in trouble. The queen is attacked and if he moves it away then 1 ... Qxg2 mate follows. This is an example of a skewer. However, White has a trick of his own – he plays **1 Qxb7!** and after **1 ... Rxb7 2 Re8** is mate. Black does not have to capture the white queen after 1 Qxb7, but he has lost a piece and White should win easily.

As we know, a pawn can promote to a queen and this can also sometimes be used to create a back rank mate. Here is an example.

Black has an unstoppable mate threat on g2, but White gets in first with the clever **1 Rb8+! Bxb8 2 d8Q** checkmate.

using the queen

The queen is the most powerful piece. If the queen gets near the opposing king, it can spell serious trouble.

White has given up a piece but now plays the decisive **1 Qh5**, and the queen and knight combine to threaten 2 Qh7 mate. Black can try to make room for the king with 1 ... Re8 but this fails to 2 Qh7+ Kf8 3 Qh8 mate. Black's only chance after **1 Qh5** is **1 ... Qxg5 2 Qxg5** but then White will win with the extra material.

The white pawn on f6 is a real problem for Black. If White could get the queen to the g7 square – it would be checkmate. White starts with **1 Qh6**, threating 2 Qg7 mate. Black's only chance is to defend this square with **1 ... Ne6**. Now White continues with **2 Rh3** and suddenly the h7-square cannot be protected and white crashes through. Note that 2 ... Nf8 – which does protect h7 – allows 3 Qg7 mate.

what you need to know

It is very important to get a good feel for checkmating positions. Always look at chess puzzles in newspapers and magazines – they often involve simple mating ideas and doing them regularly can fine tune your skills.

If there are major pieces on the board and the opponent has a vulnerable back rank, then look for chances to get one of your rooks or queen to that rank.

If the queen gets near the king all sorts of checkmating possibilities arise.

more checkmating ideas

Here we shall look at some more simple mating positions. Then we will consider sequences which see the pieces combining to give these checkmates. All of the sequences are taken from actual games.

rook and bishop

Here is a typical way the rook and bishop can combine to give mate.

knight and rook

Here is a typical way the knight and rook can combine to force mate.

mating sequences

White needs to get rid of the defensive bishop on g7.

1 Rh8+! Bxh8
2 Rxh8 mate

Here a queen sacrifice does the trick.

1 Qxh7+! Kxh7
2 Rh3+ Kg8
3 Rh8 mate

mating sequences

White powers through on the g- and h-files.

1 Qxh7+ Rxh7
2 Rg8+ Rxg8
3 Rxg8 mate

The black knight blocks White's idea, but he finds a way to shift it.

1 Rxh5+! Nxh5
2 Rh7 mate

other patterns

There are literally hundreds of ways the pieces can combine to give mate. Here are two common ideas and sequences which exploit them.

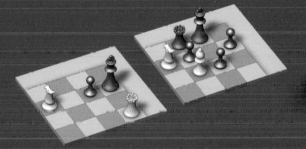

The first theme can often be set up with a queen sacrifice:

1 Ne7+ Kh8
2 Qxh7+! Kxh7
3 Rh4 mate

Here is a beautiful example of the second theme:

1 Ne7 is met by
1 ... Kh8, but instead
White plays 1 Qh6!

This threatens the familiar mate on g7. But why can't Black take the queen?

1 ... Bxh6 2 Ne7 mate
That's why!

try it yourself

Following are ten checkmating puzzles.
All are taken from actual play.

1 White to play
(Short – Biyasis,
Hastings 1980)

The white pawn
at h6 means
that Black has a
vulnerable back
rank. How can
White exploit this?

3 White to play
(Duras – Olland,
Carlsbad 1907)

Take another look at
the bishop and rook
mating combination
on page 56. How
can White arrange
this here?

2 Black to play
(Herbrechtsmeier –
Dietze, Germany1984)

The clue here is that
if the white queen
were not around
then ... Nh3 would be
mate. How can Black
arrange this?

4 Black to play
(Uhlmann – Dely,
Budapest 1962)

Another position
based on a weak
back rank. How
can Black win
at once?

5 White to play (Lasker – Steinitz, World Championship 1896)

Here you must spot a clever knight move. Notice that the black rook is pinned by the white queen.

8 White to play (Rowson – Richardson, Staffordshire 1997)

This position shows how well a pair of bishops can work together. Can you see White's idea?

6 White to play (Bistric – Gabriel, Croatia 1996)

White would like to play 1 Ne7+ but the king can run away with 1 ... Kf8. How can White improve on this?

9 White to play (Chevaldonnet – Blanc, Val Thorens 1977)

Look at the rook and knight mate on page 57. How can you arrange a similar position here?

7 Black to play (Steinsappir – Estrin, Moscow 1995)

If Black can arrange to get a major piece to White's second rank, it could be checkmate. How can this be done?

10 White to play (Haider – Kahler, Vienna 1959)

This is a difficult one. How can White combine the threats on the a1-h8 diagonal and along the h-file to force mate?

the basic principles

As we already know, every game of chess begins from the same starting position. So, it is no surprise that certain moves and patterns repeat themselves again and again. These standard ways to start the game are called openings.

Because it is often quite easy to predict the early moves of a game, openings have been studied for as long as chess has been played. Many openings have weird and wonderful names, usually taken from players who made them popular or from places where they were first played. In fact, a lot of openings are named after countries, including the English Opening, the French Defence, the Scotch Game, the Dutch Defence, the Italian Game, the Scandinavian, the Spanish Opening, the Latvian Gambit – the list goes on and on.

A huge amount of knowledge - opening theory - has built up around the openings. Many players have a favourite opening system and books on openings are very popular. At first it might seem impossible to understand such an enormous subject.

But like all things in chess, the basic ideas behind the openings are all based on simple rules. These are the most important aims in the early stage of the game:

● **Develop the pieces to useful squares.**

● **Try to gain influence in the centre.**

● **Get the king safe.**

Let us look at the starting position. At the moment all the pieces are hemmed in by the pawns and, in fact, the knights are the only pieces that can move. However, this will change very quickly.

Here is a typical sequence of moves from an opening known as the Italian Game. We can see how the three important aims are put into practice.

1 e4
White places a pawn in the centre and opens diagonals for the queen and bishop.

1 ... e5
This move is also good - for exactly the same reasons as White's first move.

2 Nf3
White develops and already we can see the advantage of having the first move. White has a threat - to capture the pawn on e5.

2 ... Nc6
Black also plays a good developing move and protects the e-pawn. There are other methods of doing this, some more successful than others:

a. 2 ... d6. This is known as Philidor's Defence and there is nothing wrong with it, even though the dark-squared bishop is a bit blocked by the pawn move.

b. 2 ... Bd6. No serious player would make this move. The problem is that it blocks the d-pawn and if the d-pawn cannot move it will be difficult for Black to get the c8-bishop into the game

c. 2 ... Qe7 or 2 ... Qf6. It is usually (but not always) bad to move the queen early in the game. If you bring your queen out too early it can be easy for your opponent to attack it with his minor pieces.

3 Bc4
This is another excellent developing move. The bishop is in the centre and White is already preparing to castle on the kingside and get his king to safety.

3 ... Bc5
Black copies White's idea.

Both sides have started the game well.

what you need to know
Activate your pieces quickly. You need to make some pawn moves to open up lines, but not too many – concentrate on getting the pieces into play.

Don't bring the queen and rooks out into the game too early. You might be giving a target to your opponent's minor pieces.

Try to build up a strong point in the centre. If you cannot do this, then at least make sure your pieces have some control over what is happening in the centre.

Get your king to safety as quickly as possible. The best way to do this is usually by castling. If your opponent is slow to get his king safe, then look for chances to punish him with a quick attack.

what not to do

In the last section we saw the players both playing good, sound opening moves. Here we will look at what can happen if you don't follow solid principles.

1 e4 e5 2 Qh5

New chess players are often very keen on moves like this. The most powerful piece is thrust into the game and, as a bonus, White already has a threat - Qxe5+.

2 ... Nc6

But Black copes with the threat easily and makes a sensible developing move.

3 Nf3

White attacks the e-pawn again.

3 ... Nf6

Now the white queen's problem really begins to show. White has no time to capture the black e-pawn and has to waste moves to save his queen.

4 Qh4

White has to protect the e-pawn.

4 ... Be7

Another very sensible move from Black. A piece is developed and the bishop is looking towards the white queen. If the knight on f6 moves now, then he will uncover an attack on the queen.

5 Na3

A poor move. The knight on the edge has little influence on the centre. 5 Nc3 is much better, giving more support to the e-pawn.

5 ... d5

White's forces are badly scattered and so Black, very sensibly, decides to play in the centre.

5 ... d6 would have been all right, but this move is more dynamic.

6 exd5 Nxd5 7 Qg3
The queen was threatened.

7 ... 0-0

Look how much better Black has played.

- Black has nearly all his pieces in play. White has hardly any.

- The black king has castled into a safe position. White's king is stuck in the centre.

- Black has a piece and a pawn safely in the centre of the board. White has no control in the centre at all.

There is already a chance for a tactic, showing the weakness of White's position.

8 Nxe5
seems to win a pawn, but it backfires badly after
8 ... Nxe5 9 Qxe5 Bxa3 10 bxa3 Re8

The white queen is pinned – a complete disaster, and all because of White's terrible development.

Let us go back to the position after **7 ... 0-0**

8 b3
White wants to develop the c1-bishop on b2 but this is too slow.

8 ... e4 9 Ng1
Again there is a tactic in the position. If 9 Ne5 Nxe5 10 Qxe5 Bf6 and the rook on a1 is skewered. So White has to make a miserable retreat, sending his knight back to its starting square.

9 ... Bh4!
A nasty surprise for White – the queen is trapped! Even though the position is very open, his queen has no safe squares.

As you see, all the tactics in this position were on Black's side, as he was quickly rewarded for his sensible opening play.

king pawn openings

Here we will look at some defences to White's most common opening move: **1 e4**.

the French Defence

1 e4 e6

Instead of playing 1 ... e5 to get a foothold in the centre, Black wants to move his d-pawn. But if he played it straightaway, 1 ... d5, then White could capture it with 2 exd5. Black would have to recapture with 2 ... Qxd5 and bring his queen into the game far too early.

In fact, this opening (**1 ... d5**) can be played - it is called the Scandinavian Defence - but it is tricky to handle and not advised for beginners!

2 d4
As Black has not done anything to stop it, White can put two strong pawns side by side in the centre.

2 ... d5
There are many ways the game can develop from this position. Here is one of them.

3 Nc3 Nf6 4 e5 Nfd7 5 f4 c5

The position is balanced. Both sides have one piece in play and both have a hold in the centre. White has more space but Black can develop easily with moves like... **Nc6** and ... **Qb6**, putting pressure on the white centre.

the Sicilian Defence

1 e4 c5

This is the most popular reply to 1 e4 and has been a great favourite of almost every world champion.

Black stops White from building a pawn centre with e4 and d4 (**2 d4** is met by **2 ... cxd4** and White has to recapture with his queen, bringing her out too early).

2 Nf3 d6

Again, there are many different ways that the game can go from here. One of them goes like this:

3 d4 cxd4 4 Nxd4 Nf6 5 Nc3

As you will have seen, the white e-pawn was threatened.

5 ... e6

The different paths an opening can take are called "variations" and "sub-variations". This line of the Sicilian defence is called the Scheveningen Variation.

It gives White more space and easy development for his pieces, but Black has a very solid position with his pawns controlling important central squares.

Caro–Kann Defence

1 e4 c6

Black has the same idea as in the French Defence. He wants to create a strong point in the centre with ...d5 and so he begins by supporting this square.

2 d4 d5

Again, there are literally hundreds of different ways that play can develop. Let us look at one.

3 Nc3 dxe4 4 Nxe4 Bf5

Black gains time by attacking the knight...

5 Ng3

... and White gains time by attacking the bishop.

5 ... Bg6

Both sides have made a good start. White can get his pieces out more easily, but Black will soon play ... e6, which will let his kingside pieces develop.

queen pawn openings

We will now look at some defences to White's opening move 1 d4 – a move almost as popular as 1 e4.

the Queen's Gambit Declined

1 d4 d5

This is the same idea as 1 e4 e5, but played on the queenside, a solid and sensible move by Black.

2 c4

2 Nc3, called the Veresov Opening, is a natural move here but it blocks White's own c-pawn. In d4 openings, White usually prefers to keep the c-pawn free, as bringing it to c4 puts early pressure on the black centre.

2 ... e6

Another solid reply. 2 ... c6 (the Slav Defence) and 2 ... dxc4 (the Queen's Gambit Accepted) are also fine for Black. However 2 ... Nf6 is not so good. After 3 exd5 Nxd5 4 e4 White has set up a powerful pawn centre and has gained time by attacking the black knight.

3 Nc3 Nf6 4 Nf3 Be7 5 Bg5

White has more space and is slightly ahead in development but Black is very solid - a typical balance in this opening.

Nimzo-Indian Defence

1 d4 Nf6

This is another way to stop 2 e4.

2 c4 e6 3 Nc3

Now Black must be careful.

White is threatening to play 4 e4, which would give him a huge centre.

3 ... Bb4

Black pins the white knight and prevents e4. He is also now very close to gettting his king to safety with ... 0-0.

The Nimzo-Indian Defence is named after Aaron Nimzowitsch who was a great player in the 1920s and 1930s although he never became world champion.

King's Indian Defence

Finally we will take a look at an opening which seems to break all the rules.

1 d4 Nf6 2 c4 g6 3 Nc3 Bg7 4 e4 d6

You remember how important it is to get influence early on in the centre? Well, this opening seems to go completely against that advice!

Black has let White set up a magnificent centre and has made no attempt to challenge it.

But Black will move into the centre very soon, with the advance ... e7-e5 or possibly ... c7-c5. Sometimes you can let your opponent control the centre in the early stages of the game. Remember, though, you must have a very clear plan to fight back there before too long – otherwise you will just get squashed!

The King's Indian is a very popular and playable opening but you need to know how to handle it.

try it yourself

Here are some puzzles to test how well you understand opening play. Some of the answers depend on spotting some basic tactics. So, think carefully about the important opening principles we have seen, but keep an eye out for tactics as well.

1 The opening
1 e4 d5
2 exd5 Qxd5
3 Nc3 is playable for Black even though the queen is brought out early. But now Black must find a good square for the queen.

Of the following tries, three are okay, two are poor and one is a disaster. Which is which?

a. 3 ... Qd8
b. 3 ... Qd7
c. 3 ... Qd6
d. 3 ... Qc6
e. 3 ... Qg5
f. 3 ... Qa5

2 The position arises from the French Defence:
1 e4 e6 2 d4 d5
3 Nc3 dxe4
4 Nxe4 Nf6.
Black has challenged the white knight with his own.

If White decides to retreat the knight, which moves are good:
a. 5 Nc3
b. 5 Nd2
c. 5 Ng3

3 This puzzle uses the same position as puzzle number **2**. White could also defend the knight. What do you think of the following ideas for White:

a. 5 Bd3 - is it a good move and does this allow **5 ... Qxd4?**

b. 5 Qd3 - is this a good move?

c. 5 f3 - is this a good move and what can Black play after **5 ... Nxe4 6 dxe4?**

4 This position was reached after 1 c4 (the English Opening) 1 ... e5 2 Nc3 Nf6 3 Nf3. Now the black e-pawn is attacked. Two of the following tries for Black are good and two not so good.

Which are which?

a. 3 ... Nc6
b. 3 ... d6
c. 3 ... Bd6
d. 3 ... Qe7

5 This puzzle uses a similar position to puzzle number **4**. Black could now try to be more ambitious with 3 ... e4 attacking the white knight. Which of the following moves is now best?

a. 4 Ng1 - retreating the knight.
b. 4 Ng5 - attacking the e-pawn.
c. 4 Ne5 - putting the knight in the centre.
d. 4 Nd4 - also putting the knight in the centre.

Think about how Black might reply to these moves.

king and queen v king

This is the most basic endgame of all and you must know how to win it. There are three elements to the winning process:

- Activate your pieces.

- Force the opposing king back to the edge of the board.

- Set up a checkmating position.

The following are typical mating positions:

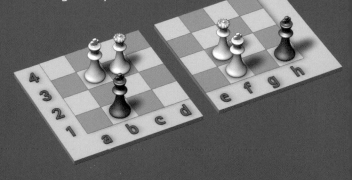

The main error made by beginners in this endgame is to accidentally give stalemate. As we saw earlier, stalemate – which occurs when one side has no legal moves – results in a draw. Here are two examples of stalemate with king and queen:

what you need to know

King and Queen versus King is the most common 'simple' endgame. It is an easy win – but you MUST know how to win it.

The lone king can only be mated on the edge of the board.

It is often easier to drive the king back with 'restricting' moves rather than checking moves.

Watch out for stalemate!

Let us look at an example of this endgame in practice.

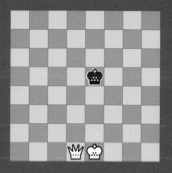

First of all, White must activate his pieces.

1 Ke2 Kf5
2 Ke3 Ke5
3 Qa4 Kd5

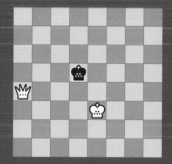

The black king is sitting happily in the middle of the board. It is not possible to give checkmate unless you can drive the king to the side of the board – so this is the next step.

4 Qb5+

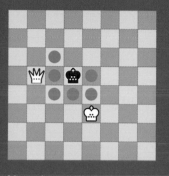

Note how all the marked squares are covered by the white pieces. The black king is forced to retreat.

4 ... Ke6 5 Ke4 Kf6
6 Qc6+ Kg5 7 Qe6

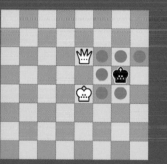

The white pieces are covering key squares and the black king is forced back yet again. Note that White's move is not a check. It is often easier to drive back the king by covering squares rather than giving check.

7 ... Kh4 8 Kf4 Kh5

Now White must be very careful. What is the best move? 9 Qd6

I hope you didn't play 9 Qf6 which is stalemate and a draw!

Instead White plays a clever waiting move. Now Black has only one move.

9 ... Kh4 10 Qh6 checkmate

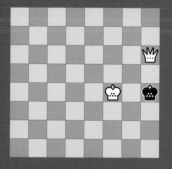

Mission accomplished!

king and rook v king

Along with king and queen versus king, the endgame of king and rook versus king is also of great importance. The king and rook can always force checkmate and it is important that you know how.

The reason that rook and king versus king is important is that rook endgames occur frequently in chess. If you can win the opponent's rook – usually by forcing the rook to give itself up for a dangerous pawn close to promotion – then you will very likely arrive at the endgame of king and rook versus king.

The steps to win this endgame are exactly the same as for king and queen versus king.

- **Activate your pieces.**
- **Force the opposing king back to the edge of the board.**
- **Set up a checkmating position.**

The following are typical mating positions:

As with the queen endgame, it is not possible to force checkmate on the open board – you must force the king to the edge.

The key idea to force mate is a quiet move with the rook. The following position is typical. White waits with 1 Rd2. Now **1 ... Kb8** is forced and then **2 Rd8** is mate.

what you need to know

King and Rook versus King is an endgame which can often arise. It is quite an easy win, but you must learn the correct method.

The lone king can only be mated on the edge of the board.

Always try to keep the black king in a 'box' while you are driving it back.

When the opponent's king is on the edge and your own king is near, a quiet move with the rook is often the way to force checkmate.

Let us look at an example of this endgame in practice.

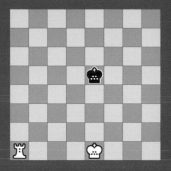

First of all, White must activate his pieces.

1 Ke2 Kd5 2 Ke3 Ke5
Black tries to keep the king in the middle, but he is soon forced back.

3 Ra5+

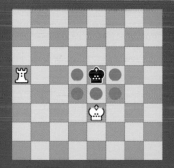

This is an important move. Note how the squares for the black king to maintain its position are covered by the white pieces. So the black king is forced back.

3 ... Ke6 4 Ke4 Kd6
This is an important moment. If White now checks as before with 5 Ra6+ Black replies 5 ... Kc5 and the king is wriggling out. Instead White now 'locks' the black king in a 'box'.

5 Re5
Note how the black king is now restricted.

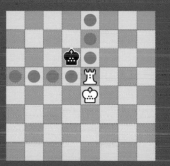

5 ... Kc6 6 Rd5

White makes the 'box' even smaller.

6 ... Kc7 7 Kd4 Kc6 8 Kc4 Kc7

Note that 9 Rd6, attempting to continue with the 'box' strategy would be a terrible mistake. The rook is not protected by the king and after 9 ... Kxd6 the game is a draw! Instead White can bring up the king.

9 Kc5 Kb7 10 Rd7+

10 ... Kc8

If 10 ... Ka6 White uses the 'quiet move' idea –
11 Rg7 Ka5
12 Ra7 matc.

11 Kc6 Kb8
12 Kb6 Kc8
13 Rd3

Again the quiet move.

13 ... Kb8
14 Rd8 checkmate

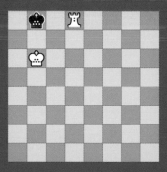

Mission accomplished!

king and pawn v king

pawn endgames

Sometimes all the pieces can be exchanged and we are left with just the kings and pawn(s). There are various rules which you must know which indicate which of these endgames can be won and which are just draws. It is highly unlikely that one side will be able to force a checkmate with just the pawns but remember that a pawn can promote to a queen and, as we have seen, king and queen can easily checkmate a lone king.

what you need to know

The endgame with king and pawn versus king requires accurate handling. You must now how to draw it when you are defending and how you can win when you have the pawn.

If you are defending and have to retreat the king, stay directly in front of the pawn.

If you attacking and the opposing king has been driven back, try to get in front of your own pawn.

If the pawn is on the wing (on the a- or h-files) there are no chances to win if the black king is near.

a drawn position

This endgame is often a draw, especially if the defending king is situated in front of the lone pawn. The reason is the following position.

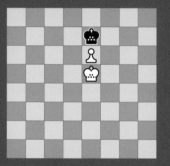

Black now plays the careful move...

1 ... Ke8

Not 1 ... Kd8 2 Kd6 Ke8 3 e7 Kf7 4 Kd7 when the black king has been levered away from the crucial e8-square and the white pawn will promote.

If you have to retreat your king, the best chance is to keep directly in front of the opposing pawn.

2 Kd6 Kd8

Not 2 … Kf8 3 Kd7 and
the pawn will go through.

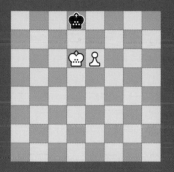

Now White must advance
the pawn. So...

3 e7+ Ke8

White now has only one move.

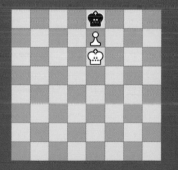

4 Ke6

But now Black has no moves.
The white king controls d7, e7
and f7 and the white pawn
controls d8 and f8. The position
is stalemate and a draw.

a winning position

In order to force promotion,
the white king must be more
actively placed, as in the
following diagram.

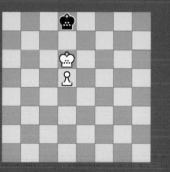

If White can get the king in
front of the pawn like this,
the endgame is always a win,
regardless of who is to move.

with black to play

1 … Kc8 2 Ke7 and the pawn
will go through.

with white to play

**1 Kc6 Kc8 2 d6 Kd8 3 d7 Ke7
4 Kc7** and again the pawn
promotes.

It is very important to
understand this principle so
that you make the right move
in the following position.

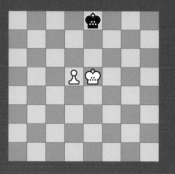

Here White can win either
1 Ke6 or **1 Kd6** but not 1 d6.

a– and h– pawns

The endgame with king and
a-pawn (or h-pawn) versus king
is always a draw if the defending
king can get anywhere near
the promotion square. Because
the play is more 'cramped' on
the side of the board there are
not even any chances for the
defender to go wrong.

With a pawn away from the edge,
White would now win by moving
the king to the side, forcing the
black king out. Here, however,
1 Kb6 is just stalemate.

further endgame ideas

piece and pawn v king

If you have a piece and a pawn against a lone king, and there is no danger of losing one of these units at once, then you can almost always win. The piece can be used to prise the opposing king away from the promotion square of the pawn. Here is an example.

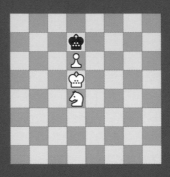

The extra piece makes it easy to force the pawn through.

1 Ke5 Kd8 2 Ke6 Ke8 3 d7+ Kd8 4 Nc6+

Not 4 Kd6 or 4 Nb5 both of which are stalemate!

After 4 Nc6+ the pawn promotes next move.

There is only one exception to this rule and it concerns a wing pawn (on the a- or h-files) assisted by a bishop. If the bishop controls the promotion square of the pawn, then the position is a win but, if not, then it is a draw.

what you need to know

You can nearly always win with a piece and pawn against a king. As usual in these endgames, the main problem to watch out for is stalemate.

An exception is with an a- or h-pawn and the 'wrong' coloured bishop. This endgame cannot be won if the defending king reaches the corner.

Endgames with two extra pawns are almost always winning. In king and pawn endgames, the pawns can often 'protect' each other even if their own king is far away.

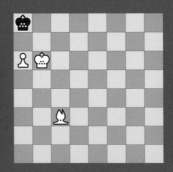

So White can never win this position. Any attempts to make progress lead to stalemate. Try it and see!

two extra pawns

Endgames where one side has two extra pawns are almost always winning. This is especially true in king and pawn endgames. The following two examples show ideas that are important here.

It is Black to play. It looks as though the king may be able to gobble up the pawns before White's king comes across.

1 ... Kc5
Threatening the pawns. However...
2 a6
2 b6 also works.
2 ... Kb6
Not 2 ... Kxb5 3 a7 and the pawn promotes.

Now the pawns are stuck but White will win easily by bringing the king over to shepherd the pawns through. As we have seen, Black can never take the pawn on b5.

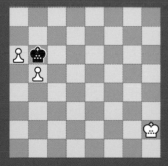

Here the white pawns protected each other as they were on adjacent files, but even if they are split, this can still work.

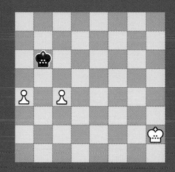

1 ... Ka5
Now it looks as if the king will mop up the pawns, e.g. 2 Kg2 Kxa4 3 c5 Kb5 with a draw.

However...

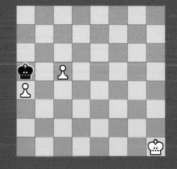

2 c5

Now if 2 ... Kxa4 3 c6 and the pawn queens. As long as White is now careful there will be time to bring the king over.

Play can go:
2 ... Ka6 3 Kg2 Kb7

Now White must be accurate. If 4 Kf3 Kc6 and the black king really will mop up the pawns. However, White can repeat the earlier trick.

4 a5 Kc6 5 a6
And the pawns still control the black king.

try it yourself

Here are some puzzles to test your understanding of the basic endgames. Think carefully about the positions and try to get a feel for how these endgames work.

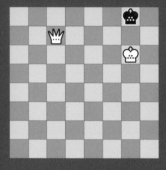

1 Here White has successfully driven back the black king and now has no less than four ways to force checkmate in one move. Find all of them.

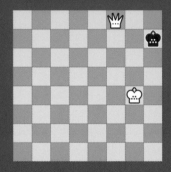

3 Which of the following moves are good for White?

a. 1 Kh5
b. 1 Kg5
c. 1 Kf5
d. 1 Qe7+
e. 1 Qf6

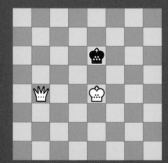

2 White needs to force back the black king. Of the following tries, two are good, one is disastrous and two are okay but do not make progress for White. Can you identify which is which?

a. 1 Qb6+
b. 1 Qd6+
c. 1 Qd4
d. 1 Kd4
e. 1 Qb5

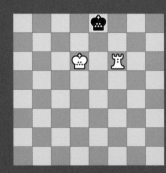

4 White has rounded up the black king and must now look for a checkmate. Which move is best?

a. 1 Re6+
b. 1 Rf7
c. 1 Rh6
d. 1 Rf5

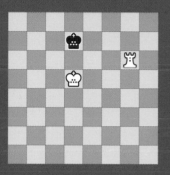 **5** What is a good move to force the black king back?

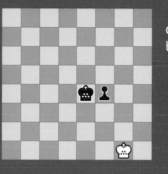 **8** White is again in danger. What is the best move here?

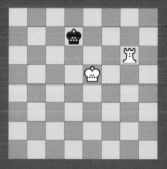 **6** White needs to restrict the black king. What is the best try: 1 Rg7+ or 1 Re6?

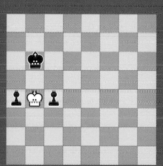 **9** White has a choice of captures: 1 Kxa4 or 1 Kxc4. One will draw and one will lose. Can you make the right decision?

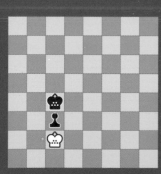 **7** White is in danger. What is the best move?

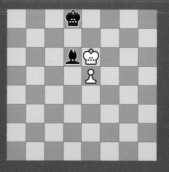 **10** White will obviously capture the black bishop here. What is the best way to do this: 1 exd6 or 1 Kxd6?

the pieces

1 a. The white bishop can move to: d4, f4, g5, f2, d2, c1. It can capture the black queen on c5.

b. The black rook can move to: g7, g5, g4, g3, g2, f6. It can capture the white pawn on h6 and the white knight on g1.

3 a. The white rook on a1, the white bishop on c1 and the black bishop on e7 all are without legal moves.

b. The three pieces with one possible move are: the white knight on b1 (a3) the black rook on f8 (e8) the black king on g8 (h8).

2 a. The white queen can move to: a3, a4, b4, b5, b6, c4, c3, d3, e3, f3, g3. It can capture the black queen on b7 and the black rook on h3.

b. The black knight can move to: e8, h5, g4. It can capture the white knight on e4 and the white bishop on d7.

4 a. The route is Be5-b2-a3.

b. The route is Nf3-h4 g6-h8.

c. The route is Re1-g1-g8-a8.

5 White:

The b4-pawn can capture on c5
The d2-pawn can move to d3 or d4 or capture on c3
The h5-pawn can move to h6.

7 White cannot castle either side – he is in check.

8 Black cannot castle kingside as this would require moving the king 'through' the f8-square which is covered by the white bishop. Black can castle queenside.

Black:

The b5-pawn can capture on a4.
The c5-pawn can capture on b4 or move to c4.
The h7-pawn can move to h6.

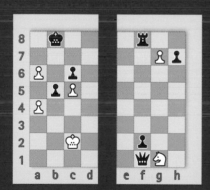

6 **a.** White can make a 'normal' capture the b5-pawn with the pawn on a4. He can also capture this pawn 'en passant' using the c5-pawn.

b. The g7-pawn can advance to g8 or capture on f8. The f2-pawn can capture on g1. Both of these moves will result in 'promotion' and the pawn will be replaced by a piece.

9 **a.** The black king is not in check.

10 **c.** The black king is in check from the white knight.

11 **b.** The white king has been checkmated.

12 **a.** Despite Black's best efforts, the white king is not in check.

tactical play

1   White can fork the black king and queen with 1Ne7+. Note that 1 Re8+ is also a fork, but an unsuccessful one as Black can simply play 1 ... Qxe8.

3   This solution to this puzzle relies on the great power of the queen. White plays 1 Qh7+ and, when the black king moves, the rook on b7 will be lost.

2   White sets up the pin with 1 Be5, pinning the black queen against the king. The queen will be lost for a mere bishop, which will give White a huge advantage. Note the bishop is protected so 1 ... Qxe5 is met by 2 dxe5.

4   At first sight 1 Bg6+, forking the king and rook, looks promising. However, this piece is not protected and Black can play 1 ... Kxg6. Much better is 1 Re5+, forking king and queen and now 1 ... Qxe5 is met by 2 dxe5.

a. The key move here is the skewer 1 Rh7+. After the black king moves the queen on c7 is lost.

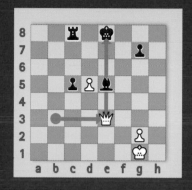

c. Here the move 1 Qe3 sets up a crushing pin. The black bishop is pinned against the king and Black has no way to protect this piece.

e. The current material balance is an unusual, and approximately equal: White has three minor pieces for the queen. However with 1 Rb7, White pins and black queen against the king and should then win easily on material.

b. White can create a winning fork here with 1 Nd6+. The black queen will be gained at the cost of just a knight.

d. 1 Bd4+ sets up a fork on the long diagonal. The black rook on b2 is lost.

f. The sneaky retreat 1 Bf2 creates a skewer. The black queen is attacked and after she moves away, the rook on a7 will be lost.

combining tactics

1 White sets up a tactic with 1 f8Q+! Kxf8 and now 2 Nd7+ forking king and rook.

3 This is another example of a skewer: 1 Rxb7! Rxb7 2 Bf3+.

5 Here 1 Rg4+ Kh8 2 Bd4 pins and wins the black queen.

2 Here the white rook picks up the black queen after 1 Rh4+ Kg6 (1 ... Kg7 is met the same way) 2 Rg4+ skewering the queen.

4 White can set up a fork with 1 Rh4+ Kg8. Now 2 Bd5+ wins the queen. Note that the e4–pawn protects the bishop.

6 This position shows how powerful the queen can be when it is near the opposing king. 1 Qh6+ Kg8 2 Qe6+ forks the king and rook on c8.

7 White must lure the black rook onto a vulnerable square with 1 a8Q+! Rxa8 and now 2 Be4+ with a nasty skewer. This combination fails if White tries to play it the other way round: after 1 Bc4+ Rxe4+ is CHECK, Black can continue 2 ... Rxa4.

9 Here 1 Rf2+ puts Black in a quandary. If the king now goes to the e-file with 1 ... Ke7 or 1 ... Ke8 then 2 Re2 pins and wins the bishop. If instead he meets 1 Rf2+ with 1 ... Kg8 then the pieces are set up for a fork: 2 Nf6+ and the bishop is again lost.

10 White is a huge amount of material down, but his knight and bishop prove too nimble for the black queen. White plays the cunning 1 Bb3+! which, at first sight, looks nonsense as Black can capture with 1 ... Qxb3. However, White then forks king and queen with 2 Nc5+. Black has two other tries after 1 Bb3+:

a. 1 ... Kf5. This also allows a fork with 2 Nd6+.

b. 1 ... Kd7. Now it is not immediately clear what White can play but the ingenious 2 Ba4! pins the queen and sets up yet another fork: 2 ... Qxa4 3 Nc5+ and again the queen is lost.

8 The key here is the vulnerable rook on e5. 1 Qc6+ is tempting, but after 1 ... Kb8 Black is OK. The right way is 1 Qg2+! and after 1 ... Kb8 2 Qg3 the rook is pinned and will be lost.

checkmate

1 1 Qxe5+! Qxe5
2 Rxf8+ Rxf8
3 Rxf8 is mate.

3 1 Qxh5+! gxh5
2 Rh6 mate.

2 1 ... Qd4+!
2 Qxd4 Nh3 mate.

4 1 ... Qg2+!
2 Rxg2 Re1+
3 Rg1 Rexg1 mate.

5 1 Nb6+! axb6
2 Qa6 mate.

8 1 Qxe6+! fxe6
2 Bg6 mate.

6 1 Qf8+! Rxf8
2 Ne7 mate.

9 1 Nf6+! Bxf6
(or Black loses the
queen – the king
and queen
are forked)
2 Qxh6+! Kxh6
3 Rh3 mate.

7 1 ... Qd2+!
2 Bxd2 Rf2+
3 Qg2 R (either) x
g2 mate.

10 White wins with
the beautiful
1 Rxh6+! Kxh6
2 Qxg7+! (not
2 Rh3+ Nh5)
2 ... Rxg7
3 Rh3+ Qh4
4 Rxh4 mate.

opening play

1 'a', 'c' and 'f' are all perfectly reasonable moves and all have been played by strong players. 3 ... Qd7 ('b') is bad because it blocks in the black minor pieces, especially the c8-bishop.

3 ... Qg5 (e') is also bad because White can now gain a lot of time by attacking the queen with 4 d4 (uncovering an attack from the c1-bishop) or 4 Nf3. 3 ... Qc6 ('d') is the disaster - 4 Bb5 pins and wins the queen!

Whoops!

2 5 Nc3 ('a') and 5 Ng3 ('c') are both fine. 5 Nd2 ('b') is wrong for two reasons: it blocks in the white pieces and Black can safely capture a pawn with 5 ... Qxd4.

5 Nd2 - a poor retreat.

3 **a.** 5 Bd3 is fine. 5 ... Qxd4 in reply is a bad blunder.

White replies 6 Bb5+, uncovering an attack against the black queen.

b. 5 Qd3 is not terrible but not very good either. The queen blocks in the f1-bishop and could also be vulnerable to threats from the black minor pieces.

c. 5 f3 is an ugly move because it doesn't develop a piece and it takes away the useful square f3 from the white knight on g1. There is a more serious tactical problem as well. After 5 ... Nxe4 6 dxe4

6 ... Qh4+ is suddenly very strong. Although it is usually wrong to develop the queen too early, here the black queen will cause chaos. If now 7 g3 then 7 ... Qxe4+ and White will lose the rook on h1.

You must always be vey careful about moving the f-pawn too early: the move Qh4+ (or Qh5+ if Black has moved the f-pawn) can be deadly.

4 3 ... Nc6 ('a') and 3 ... d6 ('b') are perfectly good. 3 ... Bd6 ('c') is bad because it blocks the black d-pawn and makes it difficult to develop the queenside pieces, especially the c8-bishop. 3 ... Qe7 ('d') is also poor, blocking in the f8-bishop.

5 **a.** 4 Ng1 is a poor move. White is just going backwards.

b. 4 Ng5 is best and lands Black in trouble with the e-pawn, which is now attacked twice. Black's only defence of this pawn is 5 ... Qe7

But now with 6 Qc2 White attacks the pawn yet again and it will be lost.

c. 4 Ne5 is a disaster for White.

After 4 ... d6, the white knight is threatened by the d-pawn and is trapped, having no safe square. Be very careful about advancing your pieces up the board too early in the game.

d. 4 Nd4 is okay for White, but not as good as 4 Ng5. If the knight is now attacked with 4 ... c5, it has two reasonable squares to move to: b3 and c2.

endgame play

1 1 Qb8, 1 Qc8, 1 Qd8 and 1 Qg7.

3 'a', 'b' and 'c' are all disastrous as they lead to stalemate straightaway. Both 'd' and 'e' will be good enough to win.

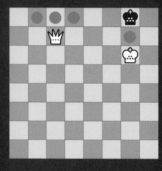

2 'a' and 'c' are good moves as they force the black king to retreat. 'd' and 'e' are okay but do not force the black king back. 'b' is an outright blunder, losing the queen at once.

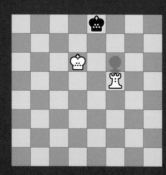

4 'a' is poor as after 1 Re6+ Kf7 the black king has temporarily escaped. 'c' suffers from the same problem: 1 Rh6 Kf7. 'b' is a disaster as 1 Rf7 allows 1 ... Kxf7. 'd' is correct, forcing checkmate after 1 Rf5 Kd8 2 Rf8. Any other retreating move by the white rook along the f-file will do the same.

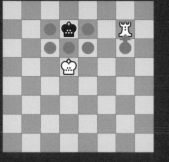

5 1 Rg7+

8 It is vital to stop the black king from moving in front of the pawn, so you have to play 1 Kf2 . White will be able to draw now .

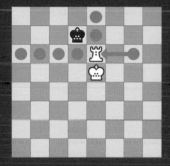

6 After 1 Rg7+ the black king squeezes out with 1 ... Kc6. 1 Re6 is better, putting the black king in a 'box'.

9 After 1 Kxc4 Black is left with a harmless a-pawn. The white king can come to a1 and then draw easily. If 1 Kxa4, then with Kc5 Black can get the king to d4, then, crucially, in front of the pawn on c3. Black can then win.

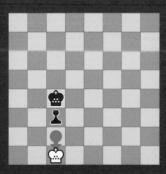

7 1 Kc1 retreats in front of the pawn, letting White escape with a draw.

10 1 exd6 is only a draw after 1 ... Ke8 2 d7+ Kd8 3 Kd6 stalemate. But 1 Kxd6 will win as White follows the key principle of keeping the king in front of the pawn: 1 Kxd6 Ke8 2 Ke6 (Not 2 e6 Kd8 and draws) 2 ... Kd8 3 Kf7 and the pawn goes through.

glossary

algebraic notation
The standard chess notation which is used in this book and also in almost all chess publications around the world.

blunder
A very bad mistake, typically one that changes the outcome of the game at once. For example it might turn a winning position into a draw or a drawn position into a loss.

castling
A move where the king moves two squares towards the rook and the rook hops over the king and lands one square beyond. This is fully explained on pages 22-23.

check
Check occurs when a king is threatened by an opposing piece. Checking is fully explained on pages 24-25.

checkmate
Checkmate occurs when a king is threatened by an opposing piece and there is no way to deal with the threat. See pages 24-25.

chess clock
A special clock which is used in almost all serious chess games. See page 33.

chess symbols
Chess annotators use symbols such as '!', '?!' etc, to indicate good or bad moves. See pages 28-31.

combination
A (clever) sequence of moves which usually results in an advantage for the player. For example, a combination might involve an immediate sacrifice of a knight in order to win the opposing queen two or three moves later.

descriptive notation
This is the old form of notation, which featured moves such as 1 Kt-KB3 and 23 QxRch. It is sometimes found in old books but is not used in any modern publications.

development
Bringing the pieces into the game in the opening stage.

doubled pawns
Two pawns on the same file (after a capture by one of the pawns).

endgame
The endgame is the final phase of the game when there are few pieces left on the board.

en passant
En passant is an unusual type of pawn capture. It is fully explained on page 19.

en prise
This refers to a piece that is under attack and vulnerable to capture. For example, if White moves a bishop to a square where it attacks the black queen, then the black queen is 'en prise'.

exchange
Exchanging occurs when both sides capture pieces, usually of the same value.
However, there is also (and slightly confusingly) a very specific meaning of 'the exchange'. Gaining a rook in return for a minor piece (knight or bishop) is known as 'winning the exchange'. The player with the extra material is then 'the exchange up'.

fianchetto
The development of a bishop on the long diagonal, e.g. on b2 or g2 (for White) and b7 or g7 (for Black).

FIDE
The World Chess Federation, based in Lausanne in Switzerland.

fifty move rule
A special rule which states that if 50 moves are played without a pawn being moved or any pieces being exchanged, the game is declared drawn.

file
A line of squares from the top to the bottom of the board. See page 7.

fork
A fork occurs when two pieces are attacked simultaneously by the same opposing piece. The fork is fully explained on pages 40–41.

gambit
A gambit refers to a sequence whereby one player gives up material speculatively for attacking chances. It nearly always refers to the opening phase of the game and many openings have the word 'gambit' in them, e.g. King's Gambit, Queen's Gambit.

grandmaster
The highest possible chess title.

international master
A very strong player but below the rank of grandmaster.

isolated pawn

A pawn which does not have any fellow pawns on adjacent files. Such a pawn cannot be protected by another pawn and can sometimes become vulnerable.

kingside

The area of the board consisting of all the squares on the e-, f-, g- and h-files. See pages 6-7.

losing on time

In any game played with a chess clock, a player who does not complete a certain number of moves within the allotted time forfeits the game and is said to have 'lost on time'.

major piece

A queen or a rook.

mate

An abbreviation for checkmate.

middlegame

The phase of the game that follows immediately after the opening.

minor piece

A bishop or a knight.

opening

The initial phase of the game. All the standard sequences to start a game have names and these are known as the openings.

opening theory

The accumulated knowledge about the openings. There is a huge amount of this theory with literally hundreds of books being published every year on the various openings.

perpetual or perpetual check

An unstoppable series of checks that usually signals a draw. See page 34.

piece

A king, queen, rook, bishop, knight or pawn. Many chess annotators, however, refer to the final category separately as pawns, for example: 'White has active pieces but weak pawns'.

pin

An attack on a piece that cannot move away without exposing a more valuable piece behind it. The pin is fully explained on pages 42-43.

promotion

An exchange of a pawn for a more powerful piece when it reaches the eighth rank. Promotion is fully explained on pages 18-19.

queenside
The board area consisting of all squares on the a-, b-, c- and d-files.

rank
A line of squares running from side to side across the board. See page 7.

rating
All serious chessplayers have ratings. The international system is the Elo rating system (named after a Hungarian professor), but several countries also have their own independent rating systems. On the Elo system, the world champion is usually around 2800, a grandmaster about 2550, and an international master 2400. A strong club player would be about 2000 and a moderate strength club player about 1600.

resign
To concede defeat before reaching checkmate.

sacrifice
Deliberately giving up material for other gains.

simultaneous display
A simultaneous display occurs when a very strong player plays a number of weaker players at the same time. The boards are usually set up in a circle and the master moves from one board to the next, replying immediately to his or her opponent's moves.

skewer
An attack on a piece that cannot move off the line of attack without exposing a piece behind it. The skewer is fully explained on pages 44-45.

stalemate
Stalemate occurs when a player, whose turn it is to move and who is not in check, has no legal way of continuing. If this happens the game ends in a draw. Stalemate is fully explained on page 34.

tactics and tactical play
The hand-to-hand fighting that occurs when the pieces interact. Tactics often involve pins, forks and skewers.

trade
Another word for exchange.

under-promotion
The promotion of a pawn to a piece of lesser value then the queen. This is very rare.

zugzwang
This is a situation in which a player is obliged to make a concession as a result of having to make a move. It is of most importance in the final stages of endgames, especially king and pawn endgames.